PLANTS

SUPER COOL
SCIENCE
EXPERIMENTS:
PLANTS

by Susan H. Gray

CHERRY LAKE PUBLISHING • ANN ARBOR, MICHIGAN

CHERRY
LAKE
Publishing

A NOTE TO PARENTS AND TEACHERS: Please review the instructions for these experiments before your children do them. Be sure to help them with any experiments you do not think they can safely conduct on their own.

A NOTE TO KIDS: Be sure to ask an adult for help with these experiments when you need it. Always put your safety first!

Published in the United States of America by
Cherry Lake Publishing
Ann Arbor, Michigan
www.cherrylakepublishing.com

Content Editor: Robert Wolffe, EdD,
Professor of Teacher Education,
Bradley University, Peoria, Illinois

Book design and illustration: The Design Lab

Photo Credits: Cover and page 1, ©Adisa/Dreamstime.com; page 5,
©Stab/Dreamstime.com; page 7, ©Filipe B. Varela, used under license
from Shutterstock, Inc.; page 11, ©iStockphoto.com/wdragon; page 15,
©AP Photo/Michael Dinneen; page 16, ©Graham Prentice, used under
license from Shutterstock, Inc.; page 20, ©iStockphoto.com/sangfoto;
page 24, ©iStockphoto.com/fotogal; page 28, ©iStockphoto.com/lsannes

Library of Congress Cataloging-in-Publication Data
Gray, Susan H.
 Super cool science experiments: Plants / by Susan H. Gray.
   p. cm.—(Science explorer)
 Includes bibliographical references and index.
  ISBN-13: 978-1-60279-522-8   ISBN-10: 1-60279-522-3 (lib. bdg.)
  ISBN-13: 978-1-60279-594-5   ISBN-10: 1-60279-594-0 (pbk.)
 1. Botany—Experiments—Juvenile literature. 2.
Plants—Experiments—Juvenile literature. I. Title. II. Title: Plants.
III. Series.
 QK49.G65 2010
 580.78—dc22   2009004312

Cherry Lake Publishing would like to acknowledge the work
of The Partnership for 21st Century Skills. Please visit
www.21stcenturyskills.org for more information.

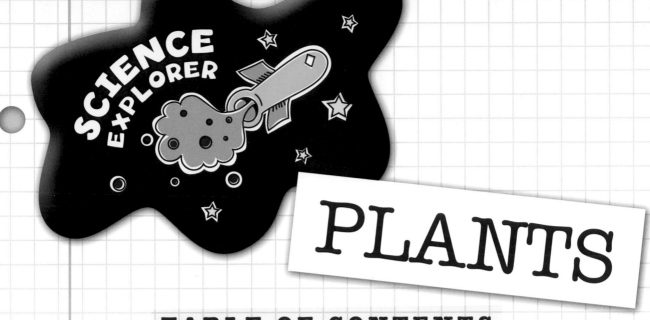

PLANTS

TABLE OF CONTENTS

Not So Creepy!

Have you ever watched a movie about a mad scientist? Was the scientist a scary person? Did the scientist do creepy experiments? Do you think that all scientists are like that?

In truth, most scientists are just normal people. Some like to study plants and animals. Others like to learn about electricity and magnetism. Still others like to invent things like superfast computers, tiny hearing aids, or lightweight cloth for parachutes. They do experiments to learn how to improve their inventions, and they know that science can be fun.

In this book, we'll follow in their footsteps. We'll learn how scientists think. We'll work with plants and do some experiments of our own.

First Things First

When scientists plan experiments, they must think very clearly. The way they think about problems is often called the scientific method. What is the scientific method? It's a step-by-step way of finding answers to specific questions. The steps don't always follow the same pattern. Sometimes scientists change their minds. The process often works something like this:

What mysteries do plants have in store for us?

Scientific method

- **Step One:** A scientist gathers the facts and makes observations about one particular thing.
- **Step Two:** The scientist comes up with a question that is not answered by all the observations and facts.
- **Step Three:** The scientist creates a hypothesis. This is a statement of what the scientist thinks is probably the answer to the question.
- **Step Four:** The scientist tests the hypothesis. He or she designs an experiment to see whether the hypothesis is correct. The scientist does the experiment and writes down what happens.
- **Step Five:** The scientist draws a conclusion based on how the experiment turned out. The conclusion might be that the hypothesis is correct. Sometimes, though, the hypothesis is not correct. In that case, the scientist might develop a new hypothesis and another experiment.

In the following experiments, we'll see the scientific method in action. We'll gather some facts and observations about plants. For each experiment, we'll develop questions and a hypothesis. Next, we'll do an actual experiment to see if our hypothesis is correct. By the end of the experiment, we should know something new about plants. Scientists, are you ready? Then let's get started!

Experiment #1
Roots and Shoots

These bean plants are just starting to grow.

Think about the things you already know about plants. You've probably made some observations without even knowing it. There's a good chance you know that many plants grow from seeds. Soon after they are planted in the soil and are watered, something amazing happens. They germinate, or sprout.

Think about what happens during germination. The root and stem both grow from the seed. But does one grow first? If so, which one? It seems like the plant would fall over if the stem, or upper part of the plant, grew first. There would be nothing to hold it into the ground. If the roots grew first, they could anchor the plant. Then the stem and leaves could grow upright.

It makes sense that the roots should start growing first. Let's do an experiment to see if that is actually the case. Come up with a hypothesis. Here's one option: **The roots of bean seeds will begin to grow before the stems do.**

Here's what you'll need:
- A marker
- 4 clear plastic cups, each with 3 holes punched into the bottom
- 4 different kinds of bean seeds. You can use dried lima beans, great northern beans, pinto beans, red beans, or kidney beans. You can find these at the grocery store.
- Potting soil
- Saucers or trays for the cups to sit in
- Water
- A warm spot, such as a sunny windowsill

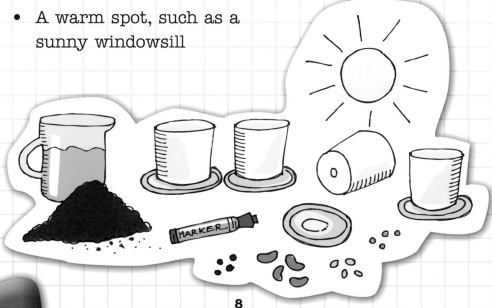

Make sure you label your cups!

Instructions:

1. Use a marker to label the cups with the names of the 4 different kinds of beans.
2. Fill the cups with potting soil.
3. In each cup, plant 4 of the same type of bean. Plant them about 1 inch (2.5 centimeters) deep. Place the beans close to the sides of the cup. This way, you can watch the seeds as they germinate.
4. Place the cups on saucers or trays.
5. Water the seeds, and set the cups in a warm spot.
6. For the rest of the experiment, keep the soil moist but not soaking wet.

Write down your observations every day.

Lima Beans

Lima Beans
Day 1:
Day 2:
Day 3:
Day 4:
Day 5:

7. Look at the plants every day, until the shoots have grown about 1 inch (2.5 cm) above the soil. Write down your observations each day. Pay attention to which part of each plant grows first. Is it the roots? The stem?

Conclusion:

What did you learn from this experiment? How many plants grew roots first? How many sprouted a stem first? Was your hypothesis correct? Was the hypothesis correct for all four of the different types of plants?

Many processes in nature just seem to make sense. For example, it makes sense that roots would begin to grow before stems do. So what's the point of testing the idea? Good scientists know that they can't always believe things just because they seem to make sense. You must do experiments to discover if those things are actually true.

Experiment #2
Light versus Dark

Corn plants need a lot of sunlight.

All living things need energy to live and grow. Plants get their energy from sunlight. But how much sunlight do plants really need? That's a question a good botanist might ask. It's also an interesting question to ask ourselves. Let's develop a hypothesis and another experiment using bean plants. Here is one possibility: **Bean plants grow best when they have sunlight all day long.** Now you can set up an experiment to test the hypothesis.

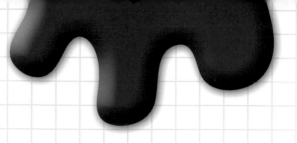

Here's what you'll need:

- A marker
- 4 cups filled with potting soil, each with 3 young bean plants growing inside them. Grow just one type of bean. The tallest plants should be no more than 2 inches (5.1 cm) tall.
- 4 saucers or trays for the cups to sit in
- A warm, sunny spot such as a windowsill
- 3 tall, empty boxes or coffee cans that are big enough to cover the cups

Make sure all the plants are about the same size.

This plant will only be uncovered when you water it.

Instructions:

1. Use the marker to label the cups "0 hours," "1 hour," "2 hours," and "All day."
2. Place the cups on the saucers or trays, and put them in a sunny spot.
3. Use the boxes or coffee cans to cover all of the cups except the "All day" cup.
4. For the next 10 days, keep the "0 hours" cup covered except when you water it.
5. Uncover the "1 hour" cup for only 1 hour each day. Uncover the "2 hours" cup for 2 hours each day. Let the "All day" cup remain uncovered. Be sure to keep the soil moist throughout the experiment.

6. Write down what you see happening to the plants each day.

Conclusion:

Which plants seem to be the healthiest after 10 days? Which ones look the sickest? How can you tell? Look at the color of the leaves. How green are they? How yellow? Which plants are the tallest? Do you think the tallest plants are the healthiest ones? Was your hypothesis correct?

When scientists do experiments, they must be careful about variables. Variables are things that affect how experiments turn out. The amount of heat, moisture, sunlight, and pollution are some variables that can affect plant growth. In a good, simple plant experiment, only one variable changes. In this experiment, the variable was the amount of sunlight the plants received. Everything else stayed the same: the type of plants used, where the plants sat, how warm they were, and so on. If too many variables change during an experiment, it can be impossible to draw a conclusion!

In Alaska, the weather is usually too cold to grow crops. But in the short summertime, farmers can grow some incredible plants. That's because the sun shines almost 24 hours a day. Alaskan farmers have earned world records for their amazing vegetables. They have grown carrots that weigh more than house cats and cabbages that weigh more than seventh-graders!

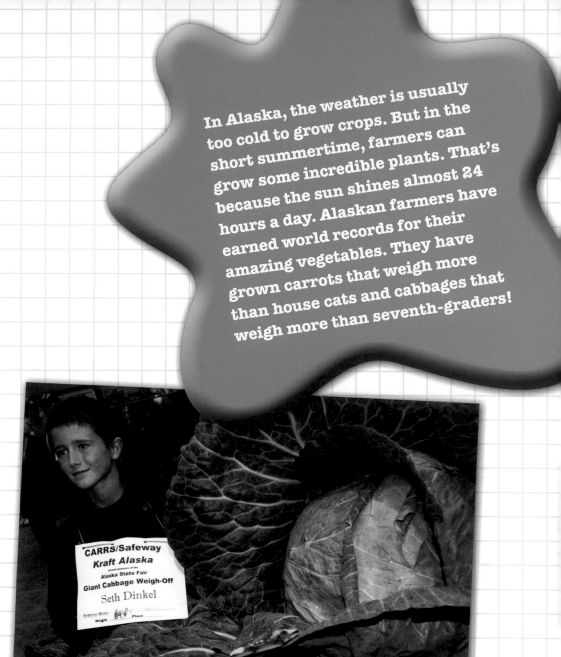

Alaskan Seth Dinkel won first place with this 89.9-pound (40.8 kilogram) cabbage!

Experiment #3
It's Not Easy Being Green

Scientists know that sunlight is made up of different colors. If you've ever seen light that has passed through an object called a prism, you've probably noticed this. You may also have seen bands of the seven visible colors of sunlight—red, orange, yellow, green, blue, indigo (deep bluish purple), and violet—in a rainbow.

Can you see all the colors in this rainbow?

You know that plants need sunlight so they can turn green and grow. But do you think plants use all seven colors of sunlight? Could plants grow better in some colors than in others? We need an experiment to figure this out. Develop a hypothesis. Or test this one: **Because plants are green, they will grow best in green light.**

Here's what you'll need:
- 3 clear, 2-liter plastic soda bottles with the top 4 inches (10.2 cm) cut off
- Sheets of deeply colored cellophane. Use 2 different colors of the sun's light, such as red or blue. Do not use green. You might be able to find colored cellophane at a flower shop or craft store.
- 1 green, 2-liter plastic soda bottle with the top 4 inches (10.2 cm) cut off
- 4 small flowerpots filled with potting soil, each with 3 young bean plants just beginning to germinate
- A warm, sunny spot
- Scissors
- Tape

Don't forget to write down your observations.

Instructions:

1. Cover one of the clear bottles with sheets of one color of cellophane. Use the scissors to trim any extra cellophane. Use the tape to keep everything in place. Pretend you are wrapping a present, and make sure the bottle is completely covered. But do not cover the opening of the bottle.
2. Do the same with another clear bottle, using a different color of cellophane.
3. Leave one bottle clear. Do not cover the green bottle, either.
4. Set all 4 flowerpots in a warm, sunny spot. Cover each one with a soda bottle.
5. For the next 2 weeks, remove the bottles only long enough to quickly water the plants when the soil becomes too dry. Write down how the plants look every day.

Conclusion:

After two weeks, which plants look the healthiest? Which ones look the sickest? Did the plants under the green bottle do the best? How can you tell? Was your hypothesis correct?

Scientists who study light probably could have predicted the results of this experiment. They know that all seven colors of light reach green plants. Those plants, however, absorb every color except green. The green light just bounces off. Green plants do not use it one bit.

All seven colors of light also hit the green bottle. While some green light bounces off and some passes through, the bottle absorbs the other six colors. So the plants under the green bottle receive only green light. They receive the one color they do not absorb and cannot use. They get no energy from the green light at all. Does this help explain your results?

The very best scientists are those who learn from many different fields. Before doing this experiment, we could have learned plenty from scientists who study light. They would have told us that green plants reflect green light and do not use it.

Experiment #4

More Than Meets the Eye

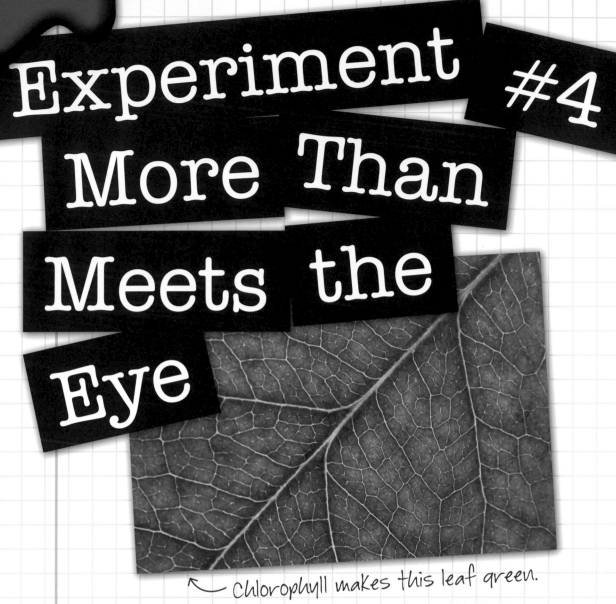

↖ Chlorophyll makes this leaf green.

Botanists say that plants contain a green pigment called chlorophyll. The chlorophyll absorbs energy from sunlight. The plant then uses this energy, along with carbon dioxide and water, to create food for itself. Chlorophyll gives plants their green color. Have you ever seen a plant that is not green? How about a dying plant? What color are its leaves? What colors do tree leaves turn in the autumn?

Do you think chlorophyll can change color? Or could there be other pigments hiding in green plants? Let's find out. Come up with a hypothesis. Here are two possible ones:

Hypothesis #1: In addition to chlorophyll, there are other pigments in plant leaves.

Hypothesis #2: Chlorophyll is the only pigment in plant leaves.

Here's what you'll need:

- 3 fresh, green leaves. Maple, oak, and sweet gum tree leaves work great. Leaves from houseplants such as peace lilies and philodendrons also work well.
- A glass jar no more than 6 inches (15.2 cm) tall
- Rubbing alcohol (This will help to draw the pigments out of the leaves.)
- Water
- Small saucepan
- A stove burner
- Scissors
- Coffee filter
- Pencil
- Tape

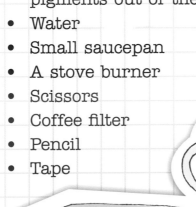

Be careful when heating the water!

Instructions:

1. Tear the leaves into small pieces, and drop them into the jar.
2. Pour enough rubbing alcohol into the jar to cover the leaves. Be careful not to get the alcohol in your eyes or inhale its fumes.
3. Add about 1 inch (2.5 cm) of water to the saucepan. Have an adult heat the water on the stove. Let the water get very hot, but not boiling.

4. Have the adult turn off the heat and place the jar into the hot water in the saucepan. Let it remain there for about 30 minutes. The alcohol should turn yellow or light green.
5. Use scissors to cut a strip of paper from the coffee filter. The strip should be about 1 inch (2.5 cm) wide and at least 6 inches (15.2 cm) long.
6. Rest a pencil across the top of the jar. Tape one end of the filter strip to the pencil so that the rest of the strip hangs down into the jar. The bottom of the strip should be just touching the alcohol.
7. Observe the filter paper as the alcohol slowly creeps up.

Conclusion:
Look for any bands of color that appear on the strip. They may be very faint. It might be easier to see the colors if you remove the paper from the jar and let it dry. Did you see any colors other than green? What does this tell you? Was your hypothesis correct?

Many plants that do not look green still contain chlorophyll. But the color of the chlorophyll is masked by other pigments.

Experiment #5
How Do
Plants Drink?

— Farmers must make sure their crops get enough water.

In your first three experiments, you had to water the plants. The plants used the water to help build tissues such as stems and leaves. But how does water get to those tissues? Do the leaves soak up moisture from the air around the damp soil? Does water enter the roots and then move up the plants?

It sounds like we need to do another experiment. Have you thought of a hypothesis? Try testing this one: **Plants draw water up the stem to the leaves.**

Here's what you'll need:
- Celery from the grocery store. Make sure several of the stalks have leaves.
- A small kitchen knife
- 2 glass jars
- Water
- Red or blue food coloring
- A warm, sunny spot
- A small spray bottle
- Some newspapers or paper towels

Do you have everything you need?

Instructions:

1. Choose 2 of the celery stalks that have several leaves. Have an adult cut the stalks near the bottom.
2. Place one stalk with the cut end down in each glass jar.
3. Pour about 1 inch (2.5 cm) of water into one of the jars.
4. Add 6 drops of food coloring. Do not add water or food coloring to the other jar.
5. Place both jars in a warm, sunny spot.
6. Fill the spray bottle with water. Add 10 drops of food coloring.
7. For the next 4 hours, check on the stalks every 15 minutes. Each time you check them, take the

stalk from the dry jar. Hold the stalk over the
newspapers or paper towels, and spray the leaves
with the colored water. Let the water drip from
the stalk onto the paper towels or newspapers.
Then place it back in its jar.

8. At the end of 4 hours, gently rinse both stalks
and their leaves.

Conclusion:

How do the leaves look? Which leaves have the
colored water in their tissues? Now take the stalk
of celery that sat in the colored water. Have an
adult cut it in half. Look at where it was cut. See the
tubes? What color are they? What does that tell us
about how leaves get their water? We used celery
stalks without roots. In nature, the roots of a plant
take in water. In many plants, the
water is then carried through
tubes in the
stem to
the leaves.
Was our
hypothesis
correct?

Florists use this trick to color flowers
for special events. For patriotic holidays
in the United States, for example, they
might want to sell red, white, and blue
carnations. But carnations are not
normally blue. To create them, florists
put white carnations in vases of blue-
colored water. Soon the flowers take
on a bright, beautiful blue color!

Experiment #6
Do It Yourself!

Does planting by moonlight affect plant growth?

Some farmers believe that certain crops do better when they are planted in the light of the full moon. They wait for a bright, clear night to plant those crops. This has been going on for hundreds of years.

What do you think of this practice? Could the farmers be correct? If people have been following this rule for many years, does that mean it must be true? The only way to know for sure is to do an experiment.

For such an experiment, what would be your hypothesis? What materials would you need? How would you run the experiment? Don't forget your variables! How would you make sure that all plants received the same amounts of air, moisture, sunlight, and warmth? How would you shield some plants from moonlight? How would you know if your "full moon" plants do better than the shielded plants?

Congratulations! You have just become the newest scientist on Earth! Perhaps you'll use your knowledge to grow the world's biggest beanstalk. Or maybe you'll create the first rainbow-colored carrots! Now that you can think like a scientist, anything is possible!

GLOSSARY

botanist (BOT-uh-nist) a scientist who studies plants

chlorophyll (KLOR-uh-fil) a green substance that gives green plants their color and uses light to produce food

conclusion (kuhn-KLOO-zhuhn) a final decision, thought, or opinion

carbon dioxide (KAR-buhn dye-OK-side) a gas that is a mixture of carbon and oxygen

germinate (JUR-muh-nate) to begin to grow roots and shoots

hypothesis (hye-POTH-uh-sihss) a logical guess of what will happen in an experiment

method (METH-uhd) a way of doing something

observations (ob-zur-VAY-shuhnz) things that are seen or noticed with one's senses

pigment (PIG-muhnt) a substance that gives color to something

variables (VAIR-ee-uh-buhlz) factors or conditions that can be changed in some way to produce meaningful outcomes in an experiment

FOR MORE INFORMATION

BOOKS

Claybourne, Anna. *Growing Plants: Plant Life Processes*. Chicago: Heinemann Library, 2008.

Cook, Trevor. *Experiments with Plants and Other Living Things*. New York: PowerKids Press, 2009.

Hoffman, Mary Ann. *Plant Experiments: What Affects Plant Growth?* New York: PowerKids Press, 2009.

WEB SITES

BBC—Science: Biology: Getting Carbon Dioxide, Light and Water

www.bbc.co.uk/schools/ks3bitesize/science/biology/green_plants_3.shtml

Learn more about how plant parts work

National Geographic Kids—Make a Cool Terrarium!

kids.nationalgeographic.com/Activities/Crafts/Miniature-garden

Find out how to turn a jar or fishbowl into a mini-garden

National Junior Horticultural Association—Experiments & Fun Activities

www.njha.org/experiments.html

For more activities involving plants

INDEX

About the Author

Susan H. Gray has a master's degree in zoology. She has written more than 100 science and reference books for children, and especially loves writing about biology. Susan also likes to garden and play the piano. She lives in Cabot, Arkansas, with her husband, Michael, and many pets.